MAKING TRACKS

MEDITATIONS ALONG
THE JOGGING TRAIL

MAKING
TRACKS

DENNIS C. BENSON

ABINGDON
NASHVILLE

MAKING TRACKS

Library of Congress Cataloging in Publication Data

BENSON, DENNIS C
    Making tracks.
    SUMMARY: The author presents a series of reflections
    and Biblical paraphrases which have enriched his life
    while running.
    1.   Meditations.   2.   Jogging. [1.   Medita-
    tions. 2.   Jogging]   I.   Title.
    BV4832.2.B437   242   79-12175

ISBN 0-687-23050-0

Scripture passages are the author's paraphrases.

MANUFACTURED BY THE PARTHENON PRESS AT
NASHVILLE, TENNESSEE, UNITED STATES OF AMERICA

Making Tracks is dedicated to Richard Loller, my friend and editor, whose honesty and courage have nudged me to hone my creativity as a risky act of faith.

Thank you, my brother.

FOREWORD

Dennis Benson is one of my favorite people. Some of my friends are quiet. They intrigue me by their mystery. Others, particularly one, remind me of a cherry on a great mound of whipped cream. I even have some intellectual friends who look like the seminary library. But Dennis smiles and talks, runs and laughs as though he were tuning in to a very special wavelength—and he is.

This jogger runs with a different gait because he does everything with a different cadence. Somewhere in the great network of neat ideas, innovative good stuff, Dennis has his wires plugged in. And I honestly believe the Lord tells him some things that the rest of us never hear.

This book is not only a fun book for the individual; it would be a super book for family devotions. For sitters and walkers and those who would rather take a nap, it still has an exciting message. For the movers, the hyperactive too, the Word comes through loud and clear.

And the Word is: Celebrate with me all those nifty items straight from the Lord who loves us and wants us to enjoy.

I hope *Making Tracks* sells like crazy because this beautiful man opens up so many new vistas of the Spirit.

Charlie Shedd

CONTENTS

MAKING TRACKS

WARMING UP

Several years ago I felt fat and sluggish. A couple of friends nudged me into a radically different life-style. One friend hinted that unless I did change I would fall over from a nervous breakdown or heart attack. Another offered his advice. They both pointed indirectly to slow long-distance running. At first it seemed like a silly suggestion. I had focused on wrestling, boxing, and weight lifting in the past. I certainly don't have the body of a typical world-class long-distance runner (134 pounds and 5'4").

Well, I have become slowly hooked on running. I am now a serious, but not necessarily good, runner. I try to run twelve to fourteen miles a day. Much has happened to me under the blessing/curse of this positive addiction. Not only has my body been challenged by the countless hours on foot, my head has also been launched into new orbits during these treks. I have had all kinds of unusual experiences. During a run I have passed through just about every emotional or mental state. Major breakthroughs in my intellectual and spiritual life have surfaced while moving along highways, fields, and parking lots.

Making Tracks contains a series of reflections that have enriched my life while I was running. This is not really a book on sports or jogging. It is about the kind of trek we must take as we meditate. There is a sense in which our past and future meet in the present during prayer and reflection.

This collection is for those who are seeking their own inner trail. The present of my running is the context in which fragments from my past are released. There are also splinters of biblical texts that seem to suggest the implications of this mixture for the future. I have drawn upon the Greek and Hebrew to construct my own broad biblical paraphrases. I invite you to accept these offerings and hope they will encourage your own probes into meditation.

"MISTER, I NEED SOME."

Marilyn, Amy, and Jill gave me an interesting gift for my birthday—a portable radio. I am trying it out. The radio headset is surprisingly light. I start to jog after tuning in my favorite FM station. Jimmy Roach is identifying the songs from the last music sweep. His deep voice seems to come out of the mid-brain area of my head, "Now some Stones."

I lengthen my short, choppy stride. It feels very good! The Rolling Stones pour into my head: "You can't always get what you wa-ant, you can't always get what you wa-ant . . ."

It felt good holding the worn leather strap as I pulled the bells. The clanging brought kids running from every direction. My summer as an ice-cream man offered many surprises. I gained more status, power, and love in that role than in any role before or after my job as a Good-Humor man.

Ice cream is to a child what the hard stuff is to a junkie. It represents the highest sensual pleasure a child can find. Kids would line up along the street waiting for me to arrive. They didn't call me ice-cream man. As I drove down the street, children would cry out, "Ice cream!" I became what I was selling!

There must be a strong oral tradition about ice-cream vendors' giving their product away. At least, I met this question everywhere I went in the city: "Any free samples?" One day I added fuel to the urban myth by doing the unexpected.

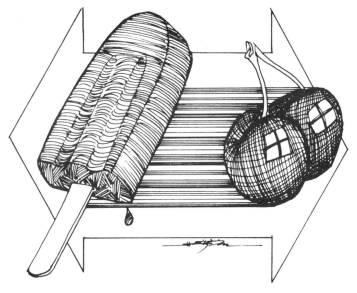

At one stop, a young fellow stood at the back of the eager crowd of customers. I finished with them and asked if anyone else wanted anything. He remained at the edge of the throng. I noticed that he had a handful of sour cherries. I remarked that I loved them. He gave them to me. I thanked him and continued to talk with the kids. Just as I was leaving, I reached into the freezer and handed him an ice-cream bar. He was astonished. He couldn't believe what had happened. "He gave me free ice cream!" The word spread through the crowd, and everyone looked at me with amazement. The myth of the free sample will live on.

Many small children wanted ice cream but were not sure how it was to be obtained. I remember rolling down a street slowly, ringing my bells one afternoon. A small child stood at the curb and waved for me to stop. He stood on the other side of the street.

"Let me see your money."

"I have a quarter."

"Let me see it." He opened his hand and showed me a small stone.

"That's not a quarter. It's a rock."

"Quarter!"

"I'm sorry." I started to drive away.

The small child ran after my truck with tears rolling down his cheeks, "Mister, I need some, I need some."

The song fades out, ". . . you get what you need."

If a child begs for food, a parent will not give a stone. (Matthew 7:9)

ROY ROGERS
—BEFORE HE
WAS A
HAMBURGER

I don't like to run on the high school track. I have to run too many laps to make my distance. I am also uncomfortable running before the scattering of students that has leaked into the stadium to get a drag from those funny-smelling cigarettes or a quick snuggle from that guy or girl. At first they laugh at me.

"Looks hard, mister. Must be difficult running with that funny gait."

I want to shoot back with my ultimate snapper, "I feel lucky to run at all since I had polio when I was younger." That line would stop them cold. However, it would be cruel and not totally true. I had polio, but it did not leave me with a handicap. I just walk and run in a funny way.

It was strange that I was visiting a hospital. I had never been around sickness very much. I guess it was the religious experience during my senior year at the University of Michigan that compelled me to reach out to help others.

I discovered Andrea by chance. She was really a neat little lady. The seven-year-old blonde had been in an iron lung for a long time. Her polio was severe, and she would spend her life in that metal sarcophagus. With great difficulty she could talk—and smile.

Each week I would drop by and rap with her. Her parents were struggling to keep her spirits strong. They said that she had a special hero. She loved Roy Rogers. So did I, before he became a hamburger chain! He and Trigger had been special fantasy characters for me. I had compiled a huge scrapbook of his life and career. I had even managed to see him at the Olympia arena in Detroit. I touched his hand from the stands!

Mother sent that scrapbook to me in Ann Arbor. I took it to Andrea and held it so that she could see it in her mirror. I will always remember the joy and wonder on her face as she carefully scanned every page. Her mother later told me that Andrea asked her to turn the pages for hours at a time.

For many hours, Roy and Trigger raced and pranced in her head. They could run and ride where she could never go. She dreamed dreams and saw visions through the characters on the pages of the old scrapbook.

Andrea is dead now.

She who rides a horse shall not save her life. (Amos 2:15)

THE CHRISTMAS TREE CAPER

From the ridge of the hill I have a view of the activity below. There is the YMCA complex, just one building and the new outdoor swimming pool. The November cold has brought new activity to the parking lot. Hundreds of Christmas trees are leaning against poles surrounding a crude house trailer. A young boy stands with his neck huddled in his coat collar. He shifts his weight to first one foot and then the other. He looks a bit puzzled as a customer holds a tree before him and asks him a question.

Herb was an interesting man. He owned a small florist's shop and grew a huge beer belly. It looked like his pants would drop off at any moment. Herb was also smart. He hired my best friend in high school, Allan. Allan is one of those rare persons who are both intelligent and clever. He had a way with growing things. Flowers, plants, trees, and people seemed to spring to life under his touch. Herb let Allan run the store. Herb would just walk around and grumble.

One Christmas the store and its adjacent lots were filled with trees. At that time the Christmas-tree business was very unstable. One season the retailer would make a fortune, and the next year everyone would have trees and no one would make money. Herb wasn't sure which kind of year it was. He had just purchased heavily.

I was in the middle of one of my periodic disagreements with my boss at the shoe store. We had parted company for the Christmas season. I knew he would want me back in a couple of weeks. However, in the meantime I needed a job. Allan talked Herb into hiring his "supersalesman" friend—me.

It is true that I had sold almost everything. But the Christmas trees at Herb's were something else. He didn't mark the prices on any of them! He quickly walked through the place pointing with both hands and shouting out prices. It was a whirl of confusion. In this fog of prices it seemed that he kept changing the amount each time he looked at a tree.

I was holding a tree for a married couple. I slowly spun it around so that they could see all sides. Herb came roaring by and asked what price I had quoted to the customers. I told him that $4.50 had been asked. He screamed at me about the tree: "This is the finest tree on the lot. It is worth twice that price. Do you think that I run a charity for loonies? It is $6.50. Not a cent less."

The young husband looked at me as Herb stormed away. "I'll take it for $4.50 as you quoted to me." I tried to explain that I had been wrong. He just kept looking at me. "You told us that it would be $4.50. That's what you promised." I sold him the tree and folded the four singles and put them and the silver into my money pouch.

I shuddered as Herb came rushing up to me. He watched the couple put the tree in the trunk of the car and drive away, then he turned to me. His eyes narrowed. "How much did you charge them for the tree?" The moment of decision. I knew that there was no receipt and that he could

not tell from the money pouch how much I had collected
for the particular tree, but—

"Four dollars and fifty cents!" Herb howled like a
wounded animal. He pulled me by the coat sleeve into his
office. He grabbed my money pouch. I was defrocked. "Do
you know how much money I owe? Do you know what
these trees will do to me?" He was shaking hands full of due
bills at me.

There was no defense. I just stood and watched him. He
finally stopped. "You are stupid, Benson, but you're
honest." With that he shoved the leather pouch stuffed
with money into my hands and stormed out of the office.

**A liar will be fired, but a truthful person will be retained.
(Proverbs 21:38)**

THE SNAKEMOBILE

The convertible roars by and two pretty young women shout a greeting to me and wave. This chance encounter brightens my tiring run. Just nine more laps to go; 10.8 miles is a long way. Time keeps rolling as I move along the blacktop. It seems like just a few minutes have passed when the red convertible comes zooming past me again. The girls slow down a bit and give me a real cheer. They seem to read my gait and know that I need the encouragement.

During college, each summer would bring a mad scramble for a good job. The best jobs were in construction. They provided the only way to make enough money to pay for school. Such a job also meant that I had to have wheels. One key to my financial survival was getting a fifty-dollar car.

It was easy to pick up one of these "transportation only" cars if I watched the papers. Dad would case the scene for me a few weeks before school's end. I would pop home and snatch up one of these rusty beauties for the summer. At the coming of the fall, I would sell it for about the same price.

I will never forget the summer I purchased the "snakemobile." It was really a fancy Kaiser. It would be a collector's item now. However, then it was merely a white elephant from a car manufacturer who didn't succeed against the Detroit competition.

It was some machine! The long, low car was first-class. It had a radically new body design. We now call it the hatchback. This made it a convertible station wagon. The most striking feature was its rich interior: snakeskin!

Each morning I would pilot my snakemobile the thirty miles to work. The left front tire was always low, and the car would stall after I had driven exactly twenty miles. Those dawn treks across town were special. It is strange how one develops a certain pattern of daily journeys. I soon noticed that the same people made left turns at the same intersections each morning as I passed. Every day the same people stood at bus stops.

We were soon waving to each other in passing. We had something in common that no one else shared. We would never speak or know more about each other than our brief encounter revealed.

The last time my snakemobile took me to work I felt a deep sadness. I would not see my fellow sojourners again. How could I say good-bye and thanks? I tried different hand signals and childlike mimes as I moved along Eight Mile Road. At first, it seemed that my travel folk were just puzzled at the strange actions of the Kaiser pilot.

Things were getting more depressing as I moved closer and closer to the Pontiac automobile plant I was helping to build. I came to an intersection where I usually passed a young woman in a gray Ford as she attempted a left turn from the opposite direction. The light caught us facing each other. She gave me her usual wave. I did my farewell mime. She looked at me intently. Then she sadly smiled and nodded. She threw me a farewell kiss and completed her left turn.

I was still sad as I completed my drive to the plant, but I felt that at least one of my mates of the road knew that I appreciated her companionship. It had been a good summer.

Falling on the sand praying, we bade farewell to one another. We sailed away, and they went back home. (Acts 21:5)

A HOP AND A SKIP

The Christmas shopping season creates havoc in the parking lot. I weave between parked cars and frustrated drivers. People don't seem very happy or pleased with their shopping. Parents are tired, and children can't handle the pressure of too many "sugar plums" dancing in their heads. Just two more days and THE day will arrive.

I am moving past the department store as a family makes its way toward me. Light snow is blowing around the parking lot. The small child keeps falling to his knees. His father is trying to keep him upright. He is crying, "I want bear, I want bear!" His elders are beyond the stage of reasoning with their offspring. The father slaps him. The winter clothing protects against the blow's force. The child begins to scream: "I want bear. I want bear!"

Christmas that year was different from others I remember. My family had a tradition of keeping Christmas presents a surprise. We were permitted to give a few selected clues, but the gift had to remain a secret until the morning of the twenty-fifth.

One particular holiday my parents were very excited about the present they had chosen for me. The hints subtly

26

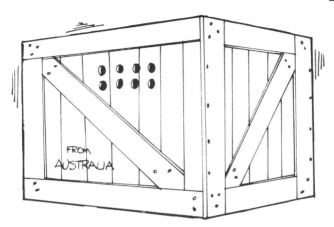

fed my imagination: "We ordered it from far away." "It will demand special skills to give it proper care." "People will gather around you when you bring it out in public."

That it would be coming by train clinched it for me. I knew what it was. It could be only one possible gift—a live kangaroo! I could just picture the impact this pet would have on my block. That kid on the next street who had always bullied me would be punched out by Herbie, my kangaroo! Perhaps I could even train him, and we could do a stage act together. What a fantastic present!

My cousin Gerald seemed quite sure that I wouldn't get such a gift. In fact, Gerald was willing to bet me a dollar that there would be no Herbie for me that year.

On Christmas Eve my Dad asked me to go next door and visit a neighbor. He was going to the train station to get my gift. When they finally told me to come home, I was instructed not to go into the garage until the next day. All through the night I could hear Herbie making restless noises. He must be anxious to know his new master. What wonderful things we would do together!

Dawn finally came, and Dad went down to light the tree. We all waited until the magic moment when we could flood downstairs to the wonders of Christmas morning. Dad seemed to take a long time. But finally the word was given, and down we came. I didn't see my kangaroo. Dad said that my special gift must be brought in from the garage. Dad left and returned moments later. I couldn't comprehend what he was offering me. There was no kangaroo, just a machine that recorded plastic disc records. I was able to hold back my tears until I reached my room. Then I cried out in huge sobs, "Oh, Herbie, I wanted you so badly."

A moment to desire, and a moment to give up; a moment to hold on, and a moment to let go. (Ecclesiastes 3:6)

SHEETS OF
SHAME

It is January already. The stores along my path have broken out in a rash of sales. A white sale in the winter! Who can think of sheets at this time of year? Yet, the department store windows beckon shoppers to stock up on sheets and pillowcases.

In the world of my childhood, a little boy who wet his bed was subjected to scorn and disgust. Fortunately, I had been able to get through that stage without much trouble. However, I will never forget one moment of shame and despair.

I was about seven years old. A special person had invited me to visit his five-acre farm. Muir Gibbs was a school teacher who handled the really tough city kids with patience and care in his high school woodworking classes. They respected and loved him. He lived out his building fantasies on weekends by running a minifarm complete with livestock and unfinished construction projects.

Mr. Gibbs invited me to spend the weekend as carpenter's helper and farm hand. It was a superworld of working, talking, and friendship. We worked hard on Saturday. I fed chickens, rabbits, dogs, and cats. I had even balanced myself as I carried a board across a pair of

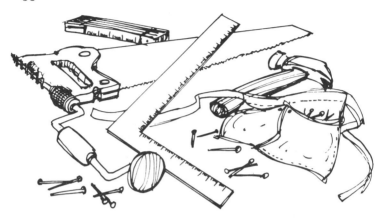

two-by-fours suspended ten feet off the ground as we worked on an unfinished garage.

I slept like the dead that night. I awakened early the next morning to see my friend sound asleep next to me in the double bed. To my horror, I discovered that the sheet on my side of the bed was soaked. So were my pajamas. I had wet the bed! I wanted to die. Seven-year-old Dennis carefully tried to wipe the bed dry with a nearby undershirt. It didn't help.

I silently dressed and left the bedroom. I kept fighting the urge to run as far away as I could. The chickens pecked at the ground and made their strangely comforting clucking sounds as I sat near the coop and cried. Finally, it became clear that I had to go back into the house and face my friend.

As I walked into the kitchen, Mr. Gibbs was slicing some of those great peaches we had picked for breakfast. He didn't seem a bit different from usual. He talked about the exciting things we would tackle during the day. "Dennis, would you get my wallet from the dresser in the bedroom?" Tears were at the corners of my eyes as I entered the dreaded scene of my sin. I couldn't believe what I saw. The bed was all messed up from the night's sleep, but the sheet was perfectly dry! Had I imagined my bed-wetting? Had a breeze miraculously dried the sheet before Mr. Gibbs awakened?

I have never told this story to anyone before now. I never talked to Mr. Gibbs about those wet sheets. Now that I am older I know what happened. He changed the sheets to preserve a little boy's dignity and self-respect. I guess that I really knew what he had done, even then.

Love keeps secret all mistakes. (Proverbs 10:12)

ON ICE

There is ice underfoot. It is foolish to run when the temperature is down to fifteen degrees. But I am not going to fight my running addiction. It feels so good to ride with it. The asphalt is a sheet of ice; so I will not be able to make my full distance. I hope my family comes back to pick me up earlier than they planned. I can hear a strange rattling sound in my ear. It is my frozen hair hitting my stocking hat! My beard is also stiff with ice. The wind is cutting into my legs. My vital parts may freeze next! I have to keep running. I hope Marilyn comes back to pick me up soon. I can't run much longer.

"I've got a story for you." Jim Symons crossed his legs as we sat on the floor across from each other. This creative teacher works as an enabler with the Eskimo people. I knew that something special could be expected. He leaned forward and related what an Eskimo pastor friend had told him.

"I was about sixteen. My father, two men, and I were fishing on the edge of the ice. One kayak was tied to the ice. The water was open. The piece of ice on which we were standing broke off, and very quickly we were pulled out into the Arctic by the currents. Along with wind and weather, it was a very serious situation.

"I remember my father's looking at us and saying, 'Don't panic, or we die.' He proceeded to get into the one kayak that was tied to the ice, and I expected to go along with my father because I often rode two in the boat. But my father looked at me and said, 'Sam, you stay here.' Of course, I didn't argue with my father, but I wondered why he would leave me out there instead of taking me back to safety with him.

"My father did make it back to the village. Some people had seen the ice break off and had rung the bell. A group of men had brought down some other kayaks. My father tied on three other boats behind him and found his way back to the ice floe. I can remember Father's coming up to the ice, and the water that splashed on him froze solid on his body. The only place it hadn't frozen was on his hands because he was pulling the double-bladed paddle.

"When Father got on the ice floe, he looked at me and said, 'Sam, you choose which kayak you want.' This was the first time in my life that Father had said, 'Sam, you choose.' Always before, I had known adults to take their choice, but this time my father said, 'Sam, you choose.' So I took the kayak that I was used to and paddled back. The two men and then my father returned.

"When we made it back to the village, I asked my father why he had left me out there. 'Why didn't you let me go back with you the first time?' My father looked at me and said, 'Sam, I looked at the other two men, and I was afraid they would panic and die. I knew that if I left my only son there, they would know that I would be back.'

"I then asked Father why he had given me the first choice. My father looked at me and said, 'You were a child. Now you are a man.' "

God so loved us that we are freely given the only son so that anyone who holds on to him shall never freeze but shall possess endless life. (John 3:16)

THE NEWS THAT FITS

The pickup truck has a blue light on the cab. The driver chews on a toothpick as he sits behind the wheel. He must be waiting for a fire to happen. Bless these folk who chase the fire engines and serve volunteer fire departments. We wouldn't be protected without them. All these adventures seem to be cut from a similar piece of cloth. This fellow's plaid shirt suggests that he must be wearing hunting boots. As I trot past him, I notice that he is playing with his CB radio. He nods to me. He looks hungry for some action.

"It is hard being new at something. The first days as a young reporter are particularly rough. You are trying to put everything you have learned from school and the movies into some kind of order. Of course, the actual job seems to have nothing to do with what the books, TV shows, and classes prepared you to expect.

"I will never forget the day when I had my first real story. I picked up the fire alarm from the police radio and was at the site as the firefighting equipment was arriving. It was terrible. The bodies were carried out of the burning building. The fire chief identified the victims as a mother and her three children. I phoned the story to my editor. In our small town, the story would be on the front page of the morning edition.

"When I returned to the office, I learned that the presses were rolling with the story, and it would be featured as the headline item. I had finally made it as a reporter. But it was then that my world fell in. My friend called from the hospital to say that the mother had not died! She was still fighting for her life. 'Four Die in Fire' was now a false headline. I told my editor the news. 'I hope to God that she dies. If she doesn't, we are disgraced.'

"I called the hospital every few minutes to see how the woman was doing. It got closer and closer to the time when the papers would hit the street.

"Finally my friend gave me the word that the mother had just died. I ran into the newsroom and shouted the message, 'She is dead!' The people in the room stood and broke into applause."

Mike slowly shook his head as he remembered his first story. "It is a hell of a heartless business sometimes."

A truthful reporter preserves lives, but a gossipy writer is a destroyer." (Proverbs 14:25)

WHAT MASKED MAN?

My daughters, Amy and Jill, are running with me today. It is really fun to have these special folk in my world. They run so naturally. We are at the east end of the huge parking area when we all notice two older women standing outside a car. They are greatly distressed.

"Excuse me, will you help us?"

We trot to a stop.

"I can't seem to make the key turn in the ignition."

It is true that I know almost nothing about cars. However, I immediately know what this trouble is. I jump into the car and turn the steering wheel left and right until it locks. I turn the key, and the car surges to life. I am out of the car in a second, and the girls and I are back on our run.

"Thanks, stranger."

It was the Lone Ranger period of my life. I was a student at a large university. Every weekend I hitchhiked to a small town. As I rolled closer to the city limits, something strange happened. I lost my immaturity, insecurity, and insensitivity to others. Even my pimples faded. At least, in the eyes of the young people in the community I took on special attributes. As youth worker in the small church, I was someone powerful and wonderful. I belonged totally to them. Their pain, loneliness, family problems, and dreams became the real focus of my life.

We spent a lot of time hanging out with one another. Perhaps it was the closeness in age, or maybe I needed their love as much as they needed mine. I was able to help these dear friends in less direct ways also. The adults trusted me. It was, therefore, quite easy for me to gather enough resources to hold the weekly community dance. There had been nothing for the teen-agers to do before this creation of mine came into being.

Two hundred kids turned out for the first event. Some of the gang came a bit high. Old resentments between certain folk flared, and we soon had an ugly fight developing. Two boys pushed each other around in the center of the dance floor. Then before anyone could lift a hand, there was a knife in Tom's hand. He was waving it menacingly at his opponent. A tense crowd surrounded the two combatants.

Pushing my way through the crowd, I went to the rescue. Without a thought, I stepped between the boys. The knife pointed at me instead of George. I asked for the knife, and

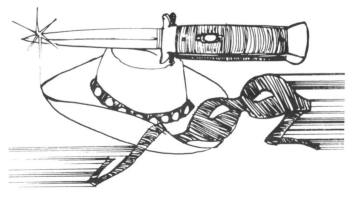

Tom handed it to me and walked away. It was only later that my body experienced the fear of that moment. It was hard to breathe, and my heart beat rapidly. What had I done? Was I crazy? I could have been killed. I guess that the love of the kids magically transformed me into the Lone Ranger.

Hostility creates a rumble, but love shields against blades of anger. (Proverbs 10:12)

ABBY'S ROAD

It is always hard to cross the places where cars must turn. I don't want to stop. So I must gauge the turn just right. This turn isn't working out right. I have to jump up on the curb and run down the sidewalk for several yards. A young girl pushing a shopping cart passes me. The smell of my own sweat is suddenly replaced by a special scent. She reminds me of someone from long ago.

I still get a funny feeling in my stomach when I think about Abby. She was the first girl I ever loved. There was something about her face, her lips, her eyes. It was just so good to be around her.

It was strange how quiet she was. I would always talk, and she would just look at me. I wanted to believe that she approved of me, enjoyed being with me.

She had been going out with a very popular jock for several years. Everyone in high school knew of their split. My friends couldn't believe that she would go out with me. I guess I could barely believe it myself. Yet, those three months with her were heaven. What a way to conclude my high school years!

We were going to the senior prom together. That is the one time to really blow your money. It would be an evening and morning to remember. We would dine at an expensive restaurant, then attend the dance in the gym which had been magically transformed by crepe paper and chicken wire into a wonderland. The post-dance partying would include all-night swimming at the lake as the last fling.

Three days before the dance Abby cut my heart out with her parting comments after a date. "I will not be able to go to the dance with you. I have promised Dick, and he is holding me to the promise." She kissed me gently and was gone. I sat in my dad's white Ford and felt the pain searing through me. I knew that I would be sick in my stomach. I loved her so. And it was over.

My pain turned into despair. I floored the accelerator and played speed-shifting ace as I worked through the gears roaring down Abby's road. I soon hit the eight-lane highway. The light was red, but I sped right through it. Fortunately the traffic was not heavy, and I made it to the other side of the street without an accident. Unfortunately, a black and white police car was on my tail. He turned on his flasher and flagged me over.

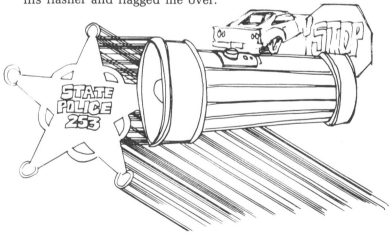

The policeman shone his light in my face. "What's wrong? Are you drunk? You nearly killed yourself." I shook my head as tears rolled down my cheeks. I really didn't care what happened to me. I told him that my girl had broken our date for the prom. His face changed. "I think I know what you are going through. I was supposed to win the best athlete award when I graduated from high school. They gave it to someone else." He looked at me for a couple of seconds. "Sit here for a few minutes, and get yourself back together. It will be better in time." He turned and left.

It did get better with time, but I still remember those warm lips, those beckoning eyes, and sometimes I even feel that sensation in my stomach.

Can a young boy blaze with infatuation without getting his jeans singed? (Proverbs 6:27)

SLIPPERY LIPS

I have seen this old Buick before. It seems to be parked day after day in front of the grocery at the time that I am running. The old man behind the wheel must be waiting for his wife. Why anyone would have two dogs in his car is beyond me. What a strange pair of pets! The huge black one leaps back and forth on the back seat. The small white one just yaps continually. Both dogs stick their head out the window as I run past. I can feel their breath on me. They are snapping and carrying on as if I didn't belong in the public street, as if they'd love to attack me. I would love to reach in and pull them out of the car by their necks!

Dad told me a story from his youth only once. It was one of those special midwest fall days. The trees were turning from green to red, orange, yellow, and brown. The ring-necked pheasant is the king of the roost in the harvested cornfields of Iowa. With a hunting dog and shotguns, Dad and his uncles were looking forward to a day of shooting.

One uncle was an especially sensitive and proud man. He had bragged a great deal about his new dog. However, the setter was young and seemed to forget everything he had been taught once he reached the farm. As the party of four men and the young boy moved across the open fields, the dog would race far ahead and flush the pheasants beyond gun range. This meant that there were no good shots.

My dad's uncle summoned the nervous dog again and again. He used all the voice commands and physical punishment he could muster. The other men in the party seemed to enjoy watching my great-uncle's embarrassment.

Finally, he turned to my teen-aged dad and asked what he recommended. The words seemed to spill from Dad's mouth without thought, "I would shoot him." Before he could correct his idle words, my great-uncle leveled his double-barreled shotgun at the dog, squeezing first one trigger, then the other. The shot patterns exploded and transformed the cowering dog into pieces of bloodied meat and fur.

With tears welling up in his eyes, the young boy turned and ran from the scene.

Biting the lip saves life, but a slip of the lip brings terror. (Proverbs 13:3)

LOVABLE RATS

The pregnant woman seems to hold onto the shopping cart rather than push it. Her face is not just tired but also worried. Just glancing at her as I flash by gives me the feeling that things aren't going very well for her.

"Dennis will be on our sales staff for the summer." The salesmen at the long table looked at me with amused expressions. I was more puzzled than they were. They looked like something out of a civilian M.A.S.H. unit. However, these odd characters did not stitch up the wounds between laughs. Their beat was selling as many new Fords as possible. Each man had his own image and his own way of selling.

Max was short and stocky. He worked the bars. He was wasted every morning. But he came in every day with a pad of leads on sales. He always played with a silver coin and could do the old Edward G. Robinson trick of flipping it across the back of his knuckles.

Buddy had a different game plan. He was the oldest of the lot. He had drifted from one dealership to another. The roving salesman seemed to be just one step ahead of a former wife or a cheated customer. His scarred face was usually hidden behind the largest pair of mirrored sunglasses I have ever seen. He loved to "low-ball" customers into buying cars they couldn't afford. He knew and used every scam.

Billy was our sales manager. It was up to him to close the deals. We would work with a customer until the moment of signing. Billy would appear and help us take the prospect over the line. He had been a professional football player and was the best judge of character I have ever met. Just one scan of the client and he knew whether to pitch pennies for a deal or to use logic.

Tall and too thin, Stan always smiled. He was easygoing and seemed to float across the floor. You suspected that a volcano was bubbling beneath the surface of his smooth exterior. Nothing seemed to bother this guy. I didn't realize how soon his "cool" would be tested.

Charlie was the biggest puzzle to me. He didn't seem to fit into this cadre of hustlers and con men. He had dropped out of school and failed at everything he tried. He looked like he was always sweating, even in our air-conditioned showroom. Charlie was the only fellow who couldn't pull his own weight. Most of his deals were "helpers." One of us would somehow be part of the sale. I didn't realize how unstable he was until later in the summer.

Life with these guys was exciting and fun. There were tricks, jokes, and continuous shoptalk. They were lively and outrageous. This team was also hard, insensitive, and unethical. I guess they were lovable rats.

Our madness and fun came to an abrupt end one afternoon. At least, it was never the same for me after that. It began when I noticed that easygoing Stan wasn't talking to Charlie.

Charlie always wanted to be my friend. He hung around my desk. I would find him looking through my papers when I came unexpectedly into the showroom. He reminded me of the kid who used to copy my test papers in Latin class. He always wanted to impress me.

One afternoon he told me a story that I thought was mere fantasy. He had asked me to go for a ride in his demonstration car. After we had driven a couple of blocks, he pulled to the side of the road. "I have to tell you something very important." I felt uneasy. I knew that I was about to hear more than I wanted to know.

"I have been living with Stan's girl, Betty. It has been great! I won her away from him."

How do you respond to something like that?

"Now she's pregnant. It is really far out."

There was a strange look in his eyes as he spoke. I don't remember what I said or did. But things had changed radically by the time I next saw Charlie.

I was sitting at my desk working on some estimates when Betty came running into the showroom. She was screaming at the top of her voice: "Stan, help me! Save me!" Stan simply turned and walked away from the pregnant girl. It was as if he had neither seen nor heard her. Charlie suddenly rushed in the front door of the showroom. Sweat covered his face. He was raving mad! Charlie was after the girl, and there was murder in his eyes. "I'll get you, you slut."

Betty slipped behind me begging me to save her. I stepped toward Charlie and tried to talk to him. He looked right through me and swung his fist at the girl. His punch missed her and hit me on the shoulder. As I reached to grab Charlie's arms, Max and Buddy caught me by the arms and pulled me from between Charlie and Betty. "It is none of your business, kid."

Charlie's next punch caught her in the head. She dropped behind the desk like a rock. He was shouting as he kicked her again and again in the stomach and chest. I struggled helplessly as the salesmen pulled me farther from the scene. Charlie finally turned and ran from the building.

After the ambulance had come and taken the battered girl away, the showroom settled back into its usual pattern. No one ever talked about that scene of horror. Charlie never returned. I learned that Betty had a miscarriage. Stan continued to smile as usual and went about his business.

I ended my summer by contracting polio. While I was in the hospital, the guys stole my raincoat and umbrella. They also wrote for themselves all the deals I had pending in my book. They were lovable, but rats.

A violent person seduces a companion and leads the friend to evil. (Proverbs 16:29)

RAW PALMS

Oregon is a fantastic place to run. The stars in the night sky seem to dangle just beyond my reach. My feet love this smooth path along the river. The path is unfamiliar, but it shouldn't give me any problem. The path turns to the right, and I find myself crossing a railroad track. I somehow miss my footing and go tumbling forward. I break my fall with my hands, and the cold asphalt tears the skin from my right palm. It is still numb from the cold, so I don't feel the hurt yet, but I see the blood oozing from the scraped flesh.

My palms tingle when I think of those summers during college. The years have not eroded the shock of the stark physical switch from studying at the university one day to shoveling clay on a construction job the next. Each of my best summer vacation periods was spent as a laborer.

These jobs meant trading the ivory tower for an entirely different world. My clean jeans were exchanged for the world's dirtiest work clothes. My sneakers gave way to huge work boots. My lily-white typing hands were reduced to a mass of blisters. I found that it was best to work the first two weeks without gloves. There were many blisters and some blood, but my skin quickly became like leather.

The biggest change was my human environment. My fellow workers spent their lives laboring. They were not just on a summer kick to get money for more education. It was ten or twenty years or maybe a lifetime of boring, mindless and exhausting work for these men. They were tough and clannish.

One summer I found myself facing five sullen faces as I climbed into the pit with my shovel—"a college kid." No one introduced himself. They just motioned toward the corner of the six-foot hole. I started digging with every bit of energy I had. It was much harder than I had imagined. I was also in worse shape than I suspected. Discarding my shirt didn't help. The heat and pain in my hands, shoulders, and arms became unbearable. Sweat burned my eyes. I could barely see a thing. "Slow down or you will kill yourself, kid." Joe handed me a paper cup. "Have some coffee, college." They laughed and showed me how I was holding the shovel wrong. I dropped the shovel and faced five smiling faces. I hate coffee, but it tasted great as I drank it. I wasn't going to miss participation in that sacramental rite of acceptance.

As often as you chew this bread and sip this cup, you share the death of the Lord, until He comes. (I Corinthians 11:26)

DON'T BE HALF SAFE

I can tell what is going to happen even though I am still three hundred feet away. A gaggle of six teen-aged girls is walking across the parking lot in front of me. Even if I slow down, we will arrive at the same spot at about the same time. They are laughing and are excited about their being in the mall. There is a sense of freshness about them. On the other hand, I am drenched in sweat after ninety minutes of running. I must smell like a neglected locker room. The group becomes silent as I run just in front of them. I imagine vividly what they are thinking.

At fourteen I decided to get a job. It was hard. I wanted to do something for which I could earn money. Sales was my field of interest. Selling shoes seemed the most natural outlet. I knew that the position paid a commission.

There were fifteen shoe stores in our town. I went to every store in pursuit of a job. I knew what I had to do. It was the manager who had to be sold on hiring me to sell.

"I am Dennis Benson. I have been selling for several years, and I have decided to make the shoe industry my field. I have looked at all the stores in this area, and your store seems to be the most promising. I would like to join your sales staff."

Most of the managers just shook their heads. "Got any experience selling shoes?" They had me. It seemed so unfair to reject a person for having no experience. How could I get experience without having a job?

I finally hit the R & S Shoe Store. The manager seemed to enjoy my pitch. He picked up a loafer and asked me to sell it to him. When I had ended my sale and was wrapping it up for the imaginary customer, Mr. Shapiro cut in: "You didn't sell shoelaces or polish! Always go for the extras just before you write up the sale."

We spent four years together. It was wild and wooly most of the time. He always pushed me hard to sell better. He knew that I would fight to the end for a sale. "I am offering anyone on the sales staff a fifteen-dollar bonus today if he or she can beat Dennis in sales."

It is fun and important to have a job you enjoy when you are young. It is the one part of your teen-age life that you can perform on your own. It is also a good feeling to share a work life with others.

The shoe business requires an unusual existence. You work hard, and you always have time for a joke. Funny things are always happening to the members of the sales staff.

Eddie was our strong man. He was dark, handsome, and had super muscles. He would play harmless games with the girls who wanted their shoes served up with a bit of romance. He would also do feats of strength. On slow days we would horse around. One such day gave Eddie an opportunity to show off his prowess. He positioned himself over the armrests of the middle chair in a row of seven metal chairs that were bolted together. After much fanfare and preparation, he lifted the whole row to his shoulders and pressed them over his head. You should have seen the expression on the faces of the two women looking at support shoes in the store window!

Helen was the woman on the staff. We liked her in a special way. She was a bit older than the rest of us. She was the "experienced" woman who at twenty knew much more about sex, life, and the world than her high school–aged male colleagues. She told us stories about her love life and shared glimpses of how women feel about things that were very mysterious and exciting to us. Being on the same sales staff made us family. She was more like a sister than a potential date.

There was one problem. Helen had body odor. I know that most people never talk about such a thing. We leave it to TV commercials. However, it is really an irritating matter when you work closely with someone. It bothers you personally, but it also worries you because you care about the person. You don't want others rejecting someone you love.

We four young salesmen met and talked about how we could do something to help Helen with this problem. No one wanted to confront her and say, "Helen, you stink." We finally formulated our plan. Each of us contributed a quarter and bought her a jar of cream deodorant. While she was with a customer, we slipped it into her purse.

An hour later we heard an angry scream. She wouldn't talk to us for two hours. However, she smelled better after that.

Spray and cream deodorants provide social acceptance, but the scent of friendship is sweeter. (Proverbs 27:9)

CALL ME
STARDUST

A colorful van moves in front of me on the inner drive of the shopping center parking lot. I know these guys. Several of the musicians inside wave and shout at me out the window. They are a local band on the way to another gig. They have thousands of dollars' worth of equipment, and they are barely hanging on to two worlds. During the day they hold down regular jobs, and at night they perform what the customers want, versions of current hits that sound just like the originals. They are trying to fight this imitation playing. They want to make it on their own. It will be so hard. So hard.

It was hard for me to get my bearings. I had stepped from my normal life into the world of magic. I was in the middle of seven days on the road with a 6-million-dollar rock'n'roll tour. The private jet, the tidal wave of fans everywhere, and the explosive excitement of entertaining fifteen thousand to twenty-five thousand people each night were heady stuff.

It was my task to interview, record, and reflect. What did the world look like from inside this magic bubble? There was little reality. We lived and acted like the royalty of old. A team of talented people sealed us off from the demands of daily life so that each night's performance would be very good.

After the gig we moved from room to room in our sealed-off portion of the motel. Partying filled a restless need to unwind and relax. During my first evening a beautiful young girl came up to me and smiled. It was easy to talk with her. She was not what I expected to find when I met a groupie. She had been invited into our bubble by a band member. The young girl was another plaything for the entertainment of the entertainers. She told me to call her Stardust.

There was something childlike about her. She flowed naturally among the members of the group seeking to bring comfort and pleasure to all.

It was early morning in Fort Wayne. I was in my room getting the tapes sorted. My door opened and Stardust entered the room closing the door behind her.

"I'm tired and confused." She dropped down on the bed. "Where am I going?"

My impulse was to tape our conversation. However, it was immediately clear that Stardust was hurting and needed a friend. She talked about her life. She had studied the flute seriously for years and wanted to be a musician.

"I had to leave my hometown. I just want to keep flying above the clouds in this magic spaceship." Stardust lit a cigarette and took a long, sad drag. "I know that it will be over soon. They don't really care for me. I'm just being used. But I do want to bring happiness to someone."

I told her that she was a gentle and kind person. It would be easy for someone to love her.

"I don't feel lovable. I have floated away from my family and real life. This rock'n'roll isn't real or kind." She cried softly. "I have been up all night. I must be strung out. I always wanted to believe that I could laugh and party my way to happiness. It just isn't possible."

We talked for a few minutes. She had high ideals about touching the lives of other people. Yet she knew that being inside the magic bubble of rock'n'roll would not let her be the person she wanted to be.

I took her to breakfast. She thanked me for our talk. We rushed to get our bags together for the next leg of the tour. I never saw her again. Nobody knew what happened to her. She just slipped away. I wonder where this bit of stardust is now. I hope that she does not burn out as she streaks across the neon sky. Stardust is rare, but very fragile in the light of day.

The quest for a life of integrity shines like dawn's light, which glows sunnier and sunnier until day has come. (Proverbs 4:18)

MOTHER'S DIME

Trucks are always a problem. But I like the drivers. They seem to understand the vulnerability of the near-naked runner. Delivery trucks always seem to crowd the narrow passages of my shopping mall's running space. Just when I am going to pass the grocery stores, there always seem to be two cars passing with no clearance. Always there is a huge truck parked at the curb. Today the Smith Packing Company is delivering "fresh meats" to the store. This red and white sign on the truck triggers something Mother told me long ago.

"Grandmother Smith was special. She understood the dreams of a little girl. When I visited her, my spirit was fed. I would dream and bask in the light of her love.

"Everything about being with her was a joy to me. She always gave me responsibility. I was particularly thrilled at being able to walk down Main Street to do my own shopping. With small purse in hand, I would spend the treasured coins Grandmother Smith had given me to buy treats.

"Mr. Marsh was the butcher. He loved children and always treated me like an adult. I would buy ten cents'

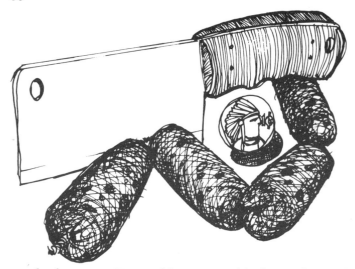

worth of sausage. He would put several links in a bag and thank me as he did his regular customers. It was so good to walk along the street and eat his freshly prepared spiced meat.

"On one such visit to Grandmother's house, I had a rude encounter at the meat market. I ordered my sausage as usual and gave Mr. Marsh my coin. He put only two sausages in the bag! I couldn't believe it. He usually gave me six or seven links. I wanted to cry out in indignation, but I wasn't confident enough to do it. I gave him the meanest look possible and stomped out of the shop slamming the door behind me.

"I sobbed with anger as I walked down the street eating my meager purchase of sausage. I told Grandmother Smith about how this adult had betrayed me. She gently counseled me to be generous in my opinion of friends. 'He is a good man. He has always been fair to you in the past. Don't reject him for one disappointment.'

"After the weekend visit I found myself back on the family farm. I was putting my things in order for the coming week when I went through my purse. I was stunned to discover that my dime was still in the change pocket. I had given the butcher a penny! Shame and sadness filled me as I recalled how angry and hateful I had been to him. He had actually given me more than a penny's worth of sausage and only gotten my rejection in return."

Don't put down others, or others will put you down. (Matthew 7:1)

THE LAST WORD

It is a super day. The sky is blue and the trees are just starting to break out with buds. My body feels strong, and there are no pains in my legs. It will be a great run! I wave at passing cars as a way of sharing my joyous spirit. A gray car slows down. Three men in their twenties are in the front seat. I smile and wave at them. The man sitting next to the passenger window raises his hand in an obscene gesture. The others yell out curses. Two beer cans are thrown out the window at me as the car screeches away.

The middle-aged insurance salesman glowed as he showed me his slides. Ted had saved for years for his trip to Africa. This visit to the mission points of the church is the highlight of his life.

The trek peaked when he spent two days with Albert Schweitzer. For years he had read about this amazing theologian, musician, and humanitarian. The Nobel Peace Prize winner had left brilliant careers in several fields to be a medical doctor in Africa.

Ted recalled the beauty and simplicity of Dr. Schweitzer as he hosted Ted and his party at his primitive hospital. Hundreds of sick people and their families surrounded the white-haired doctor as he moved gently among them.

"We went from the Schweitzer work to another medical mission several hundred miles away. This team of young doctors had been in Africa only two years. They were the products of the new school of medicine. They had the latest equipment and techniques. Their hospital was in striking contrast to that of Dr. Schweitzer's.

"We were shocked by the attitude of these young medical men. They spent most of our four hours with them attacking the primitive ways of Dr. Schweitzer. They said that he was a disgrace to medicine. There was bitterness and anger in these folk.

"Just before we left, one lady in our party said to them something that we had all felt but had been hesitant to say. She asked the doctors if she might say a word: 'We just left Dr. Schweitzer, as you know. He told us about the work you are doing. He said that he thanks God for what you are doing here. He is proud to think of you as his brothers in Christ. He prays daily for your gifts and work.'

"The three young doctors were silent. They just looked at the ground in embarrassment."

A sensitive person tells it like it is, but fools blather slander. (Proverbs 15:2)

BETWEEN THE SPROCKETS

The yellow bus is teeming with bodies and voices. Every window seems to feature countless limbs and faces. The women's track team is on the way to its first meet. I wave at them. It is their third year, and they are a great lot. I used to run with them sometimes during their practices. It is good that women now have a real chance to enjoy sports. It is painful for anyone to be left out of this realm in school.

The jocks were at the top of the social heap in our junior high school. It was hard to find a rung on the ladder if you didn't hang out in locker rooms.

I thought that I had found my place when I heard a public announcement one morning. I went to the organizing meeting of the Projection Club. We were the people who ran the movie projectors. The fifteen people in the room looked like losers to me. They were the funny kids who were shorter and had more zits than did the more popular students. It seemed that most of them wore glasses. Looking back at the scene from my perspective as an adult, I know that they were also the more intelligent kids. They were the ones who would go on to do some significant things in the technical fields.

The teacher who sponsored the club took several sessions to train us. At that time in American educational history, the audio-visual field was considered the salvation of the public school. Just aim the 16mm projector at a screen and the students will learn what they need to learn. This meant that we were cautioned about the use of the equipment. "You must be very careful never to damage the equipment. More importantly, never damage the film!"

Unfortunately, I really didn't fit into this group. I wasn't into science fiction and didn't have superior technical interest. It is true that I had more zits than normal and was short, though.

My first test as a member of the Projection Club came with the showing of a government film. About three hundred kids filed into the auditorium with its nailed-down desk chairs. I had the machine threaded and ready to roll. A certain sense of power swelled in me. You would have thought that I was the projectionist at Radio City Music Hall or something. I kept my feet in the aisle as the kids filed past me. I wanted them to see and know who was at the helm. On my shirt everyone could see the bold yellow badge, Projection Club. An automatic hall pass!

I signaled for the lights to be lowered. I switched on the Bell and Howell and let the forty-five minute film roll. The picture was fine. However, the sound was strange. The music and words growled out at us. No one complained. The teachers didn't even seem to be listening to the sound track. I kept checking and twisting knobs. The machine seemed to be working fine.

About ten minutes into the movie, I noticed that the take-up reel was completely filled. How could this be? As I looked closely at the film coming out of the projector, I realized in horror what was happening. I had misthreaded the film. The projector was systematically punching new sprocket holes between each set of existing holes! The color film was being completely ruined.

That afternoon I was asked to resign from the Projection Club. One teacher even hinted that the FBI would probably be checking up on me for having destroyed government property.

The lumpy or bumpy cannot be made smooth again. (Ecclesiastes 1:15)

HE MADE ME
DO IT

                  The dirt along the roadsides is really red! I had forgotten that this part of the South is red clay country. When I had visited this area years ago, I was more concerned about how the police were treating the civil rights marchers. I wonder if they are used to runners in this rural setting. I am passing an old house. The doorway and windows are open. It almost looks as if there are no windows or doors in the building. Chickens are casually strolling across the porch. A man sits in a rocker and peacefully watches the big attraction of a stranger running down his road. "Better be careful. You can lose weight doing that." He cackles with high-pitched laughter and unconsciously rubs his pot belly. There is a shotgun leaning against the wall to his left. He is amused rather than angered by my intrusion into his world.

                    There are disadvantages in having an uncle who is near your own age. For one thing, it makes him more advanced but without the wisdom of maturity.

An indulgent aunt gave me a bright new BB gun. Since I was only three years old, I could not cock the air rifle. My parents assumed that this lack of muscle would keep me from shooting up the countryside.

However, Uncle Walt helped me overcome this handicap. He loaded my prized BB gun and cocked it for me. What happened next is a memory blur. The family came rushing out of the house when they heard the screams from Walt. They found him bleeding from the face. A half inch over his left eye a BB had made a neat little hole. Just a slight change of direction and he would have been blinded. I was holding the "smoking" gun.

Before they rushed Walt to the hospital, my dad took the gun and smashed it over a nearby rock. The stock splintered. He took the gun by the barrel and hurled it as far as he could into the woods.

I cried and cried for my lost gun.

And they shall smash their guns into hoes and their weapons into shovels. (Isaiah 2:4)

BY THE LIGHT OF
THE MOON

*Night running is always spe-
cial. The harvest moon seems to reach out and touch me. I
keep watching it as I move along the country road. The
clouds drift across it, offering it a snuggle, and pass on.
How many other people are watching the autumn moon?*

The two men are sitting to-
gether. Ed is telling Stan the story of his relationship with
his retarded son.

"We have this special Sunday school class in which
parents and children study together. We had been looking
at nature as one means of understanding aspects of God's

love and care. My son was particularly excited about the moon.

"When he got home he told me that he wanted to go look at the moon with me. Each night something seemed to interfere to keep us from doing this. I couldn't understand why it was so important to him. We had seen the moon many times before.

"Finally, the perfect evening arrived. The moon was full and beautiful. He wanted me to sit beside him on the swing while we watched the moon together. As we were sitting there, he put his arm around me. I suddenly realized that all these years I had really rejected him because of his retardation. And here he was accepting me."

Ed sobs. Stan quietly comforts his friend.

The moon will be a constant reminder, the covenant in the night sky is forever. (Psalm 89:37)

BEANLESS
BENSON

The kids are spilling out of the Catholic grade school. It is incredible to watch the individuals and knots of people being disgorged from the bowels of academia. Free at last! I run past the many faces. It is tempting to speculate about each face. They seem so young and open. However, one little boy catches my imagination and sympathy. His tie is twisted to one side. There are tear smears on his cheeks. He is not mad or indignant. His lip quivers, and he is fighting to escape some fear or humiliation. He breaks into a run and soon vanishes into a wooded area outside the playground.

Being an only child means being a lonely child. At least, that seemed to be the case with me at certain points in my life. It is particularly hard to be an only child and new on the block. The kids in my neighborhood enjoyed intimidating me. Perhaps I was really a coward. I know that after one particular week I certainly felt like a spineless little boy.

The kids started hazing me at the beginning of school. They found great pleasure in throwing my hat into a tree. I always wore a hat that winter because I had had pneumonia twice, and in the pre-penicillin days it was a serious illness. I tried to shame the bullies into being nice to me. "My mother will have to wash the hat, and she hasn't been feeling well." A huge chorus of laughter greeted my ploy as they threw it high into a tree. "Beanless Benson, Beanless Benson, Beanless Benson."

They thought it would be fun to terrorize me. They threatened to beat me senseless after school. I ran the mile along the streets between home and school in overwhelming fear. I tried to find a different path so that I would not be caught. But no one tried to hurt me.

One day I was playing alone in my yard. Suddenly Billy appeared and hit me in the face. He knocked me down and disappeared. My fear was uncontrollable at that point. My dad tried to help me by arranging a boxing match between the bully and me. This only made me more afraid.

The match was a moment of utter disgrace. The other boy came in the ring and punched me twice. I was knocked down and afraid to get up. The other kids in the neighborhood laughed and sneered at me. "Beanless Benson, Beanless Benson, Beanless Benson." Dad gave the decision to Billy and promised that I would not have comics and other rewards for several weeks.

As I cried alone, my dog, Duke, licked my hands and seemed to care about a disgraced and flawed young boy who could neither fight nor win friends.

All day my shame and humiliation overwhelm me. (Psalm 44:16)

MISTY LADY

Sitting at my typewriter I feel guilty. I should have finished more of my writing by this time. The lawn work was a good excuse for not getting down to work earlier in the day. It is now eleven-thirty. While I am working, I know that I have not run today either. I can't break my pattern and miss a day. I should slip into my shorts and head for the track.

The summer evening is mysterious. Perhaps it is the strange weather. The fog came from nowhere and covers everything with a shroud of gray. I can't see more than a few feet in front of me.

My compulsion to run takes me to the track for a late-night jog. The intense fog transforms the track into a place of mystery. The darkness is alive with a presence that cannot be seen but is deeply felt. As I approach the oval, I know that someone else is on the track. The runner can't be seen.

Just as I step onto the track, a young woman passes by and instantly disappears into the fog. I call out a greeting and she answers.

I can hear the sound of her running shoes hitting the asphalt just ahead of me. The fog does something funny to the sound. The footsteps seem to remain locked in their original space. It is as if I were running into her sound. I strain to hear the sound of her breathing.

The mystery woman keeps ahead of me. Questions roll through my mind as I run. Running always does something strange to my mind. I dream dreams, scheme schemes, and fantasize fantasies. My imagination focuses on the lady of the mist. Why is she on the high school track at midnight? Is she lonely? What problems is she struggling with as she runs? Is there someone at home who misses her?

Are these questions in her mind, or do they exist only in my own thoughts? Are the two of us much alike because of our journey in the fog, or are we mere sojourners with a compulsion to run?

I suddenly realize that she is no longer ahead of me. She has turned off and left the track. I will never know more about her. We will never run together again. It is somehow much lonelier running without the lady of the mist.

How graceful is your stride, misty lady! (Song of Solomon 7:1)

MUDDY HANDS

The two teen-agers are laughing so hard that they can barely stand. As I draw closer to the ice-cream store, I can see the bizarre predicament that has triggered their hysteria. They are trying to eat "skyscraper" ice-cream cones. However, the ice cream is running down their hands. The front of their shirts is covered with chocolate ice cream. They are shaking their sticky hands and laughing.

Ed is proud of the tours he has organized for the folk in Brisbane. This beautiful part of Australia offers especially fine opportunities to go "out back." These wilderness treks are a delight for all. However, one trip changed Ed's view of organizing such journeys.

"I had arranged a two-bus tour. The first vehicle contained a good cross section of adults. The second bus was composed of handicapped young people and adults. We treated the groups as separate parties. All was well on the holiday outing until both buses got stuck in the same riverbed. The drivers could not drive their vehicles free of the mud.

"The travelers in the second bus immediately suggested

that they get out and push. They cheerfully began working in the water and mud to free the bus. The sighted helped the blind, and the spirit of mutual support was incredible.

"The folk in the first bus were complaining about their predicament. The driver told them that the handicapped people were trying to move their own bus. This shamed the others to help in moving the vehicles. Both parties mixed to help get each bus moving. They laughed and enjoyed the experience.

"The people decided to travel as a mixed group for the rest of the trip and not as two separate parties. When they reached the destination, the fellowship of handicapped and nonhandicapped was intense and real.

"One of the blind teen-agers said to me after our return, 'We were strangers until our hands were covered with mud. Then we became friends.' "

Jesus placed his hands on the sick woman, and at that moment she was well. (Luke 13:13)

BE-BACK BOOK

*The man didn't notice me as I
ran past him. He was totally absorbed by the sight before
him. The middle-aged man enjoyed gazing at his new car.
The price sticker was still on the window. When I sold cars,
it always amused me how a customer would fight for a
lower price while leaving the higher-priced sticker on the
window to impress the neighbors. You can't always tell the
price of a car by its sticker.*

"The first thing you do is
qualify the customer." This instruction from my sales
manager was important. You had to find out whether the
client could buy an automobile or not. If he or she were just
shopping, you have to help the person out the door as
quickly as possible. There were only so many "ups" during
your limited floor-time at the dealership.

Most of the salesmen could just glance at a person and
tell whether the person were just looking or wanted to buy a
car. You could spend an hour with some people, and just
when you reached the serious stage, he or she would say,
"I'll be back." Stan used to smile and ask if they wanted to
sign the "be-back book."

However, you can't always judge a person by looks. One

afternoon a young fellow came into the showroom. It was Buddy's up, or turn to get the customer. He looked at the boy with the Pat Boone white bucks. "A real flake. You can have him."

The boy was circling a golden Thunderbird loaded with every possible extra. "How much does it cost?" He was not disturbed by the list price. The boy's father had suffered a stroke. He had done all the negotiations to sell his dad's farm to a builder. His mother told him to buy any car he wanted.

That same afternoon I delivered the car and pocketed one of my biggest commissions that summer. Buddy just shook his head. "He sure looked like a flake to me."

Do not "qualify" a person by superficial appearances, but draw conclusions from sound qualities. (John 7:24)

REVELATION
WATER

I had missed the weather forecast. It was hot and stuffy. I couldn't shed my sweatsuit. I was on a continuous run and would not return this way today. The sweat poured from me. It was probably good for me. However, after an hour and a half my mouth was dry, and I longed for a drink. I imagined myself dizzy. Yet I couldn't help smiling. I have been thirsty before.

Bright Angel Trail. There was nothing forbidding about this simple marker. We knew that the Grand Canyon presented a challenge to those who walked to the bottom and back. Yet the three of us were young and strong. This was our journey of celebration after a hard year at college.

The ranger had told us that it was a difficult hike. We were warned that an ample supply of water was required for the descent and return.

We started at dawn. The air was bright and cold. We didn't have hiking boots nor a very good water container. I filled the plastic container we had used for washing dishes. The soapsuds immediately formed a head on our limited water supply.

The walk provided new wonders around every bend.

The shifting sunlight kept changing the colors on the canyon walls. We had read that there were water stops along the way. However, we found no water available during our day of hell.

It was noon when we reached the Colorado River. Instead of resting at the bottom of the canyon, we decided to return to the rim immediately. It was the return journey that put the pressure on us. We found ourselves walking a few feet and stumbling to our knees. At first, we laughed about our poor imitation of cheap cowboy films. However, it soon became more serious. Our mouths were dry, and we ached everywhere. Our clothes were covered with the dust and mule dung and dirt. We saw no one else on the trail that day.

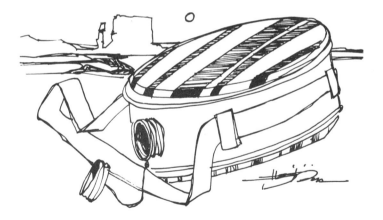

It was hard to continue. As we sat on the trail, we could see huge birds circling over us. Far above us people were on the rim with cameras. There was no way to signal our distress.

We suspected that this was the end. Suddenly a man stood in front of us. He held a large water jug. "I spotted you fellows from the rim. I could tell that you were in trouble."

We almost cried as we tasted the cool water. After a few minutes the water revived us and our rescuer helped us to the rim. I kept looking at his jug and smiling about the word printed on it: Revelation.

Whoever drinks of the water I give will not be thirsty ever again. (John 4:14)

THE PIG POT

The fat man waddled out of the village newsstand. He was licking his swollen lips as he firmly clutched the state lottery tickets he had just purchased. Visions of prizes and fame seemed to sparkle in his eyes. As I ran past him, he was getting into his car. The whole car seemed to groan as he dropped into the seat. My mind skipped back in time. I thought of Isaiah 53. What if the Messiah comes to us in the shape of one who is uncomely and fat?

"Everybody put in a dollar." I didn't know what the resident advisor was suggesting. As a new student at the University of Michigan, I wasn't used to the customs surrounding the exchange dinners. I soon learned.

Each week a women's dorm would invite a certain number of male students to visit for dinner. This was a blind-date affair. A boy was assigned to a girl. I guess this was a way of meeting people. However, everyone felt quite cynical about it.

In order to keep the system going, the resident advisor devised the "pig pot." The dozen or so guys each put a dollar in the pot. The advisor would hold the money. Upon

83

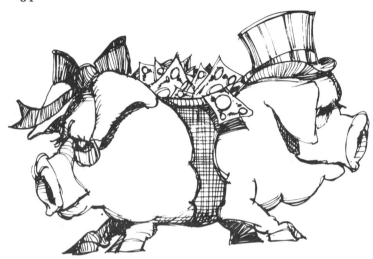

our return he would give the fund to that person who had the ugliest date. In other words, the pot would go to the fellow who got the "pig."

What a cruel and ugly system this was. It went hand in hand with the stories of a guy's calling a blind date from the lobby of the dorm and waiting for her to arrive. If she did not meet the guy's standard, he would simply leave without even speaking to her.

I found out years later that the women had also had a "pig pot." The girl with the ugliest date would win their pool.

I often wondered if I had ever been the star pig.

His figure and His appearance would not win approval from others. (Isaiah 53:2)

THE LAST GIFT

*It is raining as I start my run.
The first few miles are always the hardest. The first
awareness of my shoes' filling with cold water does not
help. A long line of headlights clearly outlines the highway
to my left. It is a funeral. The caravan rolls right through
the red light. An expensive farewell party.*

At first the stark hospital
surroundings overwhelmed me when I made my rounds.
My initial few weeks as a student chaplain were shattering.
I had never liked illness. I had never been around sick
people. Now my whole world was filled with the infirm
and dying.

"Chaplain, chaplain, come this way." The nurse quickly
filled me in on the circumstances of our destination as she
led me down the hall. An old woman was close to death
and needed some comfort. The first wave of concern was
for myself. How could I provide comfort when I was so
uncomfortable?

The woman smiled as I walked into the room. The first
sight of her drawn face told me that she was closer to the
dead than to the living. Yet I knew that I was there to care
for her.

We sat together for hours that day. She would drop off to sleep and seem far away. At other times she would be very alert. I learned much about her. She had no relatives. Her husband had died years ago. As we talked, she kept drawing more and more of my history from me. She wanted to know my dreams and concerns.

About 8:30 PM she began to look very strange. Her eyes glazed over from time to time. Her breathing shortened. At times I was afraid that she was not going to make the next breath. I knew that her time was short. She would be dead soon.

I signaled for the nurse. I was holding the dying woman's hand. She looked at me for several seconds. "Don't be afraid, Dennis. It will be all right." She died. Her life slipped away between my hands. Her last act was to give a crying young chaplain comfort.

The criminal said, "Jesus remember me when you take over." And Jesus said to him, "I assure you, today you will be with me in a better place." (Luke 23:42-43)

HAIR TRIGGER

The August heat has been oppressive. The village of Kaleva may be a Michigan version of Finland, but I missed the ice. About midnight, a breeze rises. It is my chance to hit the country roads for a run. As I move along the dirt trail, I remember the joking comment of a relative: "Be careful at night. A bear or snake might get you along one of those roads." Everyone had laughed heartily at his amusing remark. Yet, as the lights of the small town disappeared, I thought that the shadows were unusually alive. Wonder if I stepped on a snake that had come onto the road in the cool of the evening? All kinds of snake stories rattled through my imagination. Stewart Hoover's tale came floating into my head.

"I was twelve years old and just getting used to riding by myself. There were different levels of horses on my uncle's ranch. One horse was for all the little kids. However, I was old enough to ride one of the work horses. Eve was old, but she was a real range animal.

"My older brothers were able to go off to do the fun stuff. Finally, my time had come to go out and ride the fence. Fence riding was nothing as far as the older boys were concerned. They had done that for a number of years. It is really kind of boring. You ride along, and every time you see a place where the barbed wire is pulled down you get off and nail the wire up again. But you get to ride miles and miles by yourself.

"In order to keep me from feeling left out, my uncle let me take along a rifle in a saddle holster. I felt like big stuff with this loaded gun. I rode along dreaming all kinds of fantasies about being Paladin and other western characters.

"I had been riding for about two hours without much fence to repair when I came to a dry creek bed. I got to the bottom of it, and the horse stopped dead still in her tracks. I didn't know what was going on until I heard a rattling sound! It was more of a hissing sound. I saw the rattlesnake in front of us. I rose tall in the saddle. I thought: 'Here is my chance. I'll show those guys. I'll take back a rattlesnake skin.'

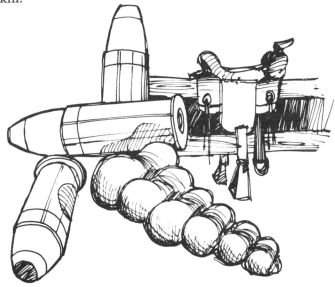

"So I pulled out the rifle. I was a little naïve. If I had known what I was doing, I would not have tried to shoot the rifle while sitting on the back of the horse like that. You never know whether a horse is used to shooting or not. The shot would have gone right by her head.

"I fumbled with the gun and finally got it out of the holster. I cocked it and was just drawing a bead on the snake's head when the horse shrugged and took one step right on the rattlesnake. Killed it instantly! I was almost as crushed as the snake. I got down and tied the snake to the saddle. I took it back and tried to tell the guys that I had killed it. However, it was pretty clear what had happened. When I told the story, my uncle explained that the wise old range mare had had experience killing snakes to protect her foal. She had known what she was doing. 'Maybe she felt that she was protecting you.' "

The man named his wife Eve, because she is the mother of all life. (Genesis 3:20)

A CLEAN MACHINE

I start across the Giant Eagle Supermarket parking lot when I spy the supervan. The owner has put everything into this motel on wheels. I know from the tour he gave me of this rolling womb that he has stereo, a TV, full carpeting, all the luxuries of home. I wave to Bill as I see him gathering carts in front of the store. I know that he is working on two jobs to pay for this symbol of the good life. At nineteen he has strapped himself into an inescapable bind. It seems I have heard his story before.

The woman was simply dressed but conveyed an impression of order. I noticed her three-year-old car as she drove up to the car dealership. She came to the point as she sat at my desk in the showroom. "I want a new car. I need a car. However, I don't have much money. In fact, I can pay only sixty-five dollars a month. I am a widow with four children. My budget will permit only that amount each month. The last time I bought a car the salesman told me that it would cost a certain amount, but when I got the payment book, the price was twenty dollars more a month. It has been very hard to meet the payments.

I had her trade-in appraised. I focused on the bottom of

the line with no accessories. However, there was no way I could touch her sixty-five-dollar-a-month payment level. I talked with the manager. We figured it every possible way. I was still twenty-five dollars a month too high. I told her the bad news. She thanked me and left.

The manager came to my desk and asked about the deal. I told him that I couldn't get it to the level she could afford; so she had left. He exploded. Was I crazy? Didn't I know that the next dealer would drop her in by "low balling" her? Why didn't I promise the deal she wanted and let her handle the higher payments when she got the book? He stormed away.

An hour later he called me into his office. "You let that woman get away. People like that will always manage to pay higher bills. I don't want a salesman like you around. You are fired, Benson."

Hold on to the truth. Do not sell it out. (Proverbs 23:23)

YOU'LL PAY, YOU BASTARD!

As I run past the grocery store, I see a teen-ager look on in shock as the shopping cart he had been guiding a moment ago rolls into the fender of a parked car. I can see the horror on the boy's face. The driver springs from the car. His face is already red. He spits out a string of curses. He slams the door of the car. His body is trembling with anger. "You'll pay, you bastard!"

My first thought is that this old man will die of a heart attack on the spot unless he is restrained. I am even with him, but I don't stop. I keep on running. Well, I can stop when I pass this spot again in twelve minutes or so. I think about this scene every step of my run. Could they get into a fist fight over this? Could someone get hurt? When I get to the top of the hill on my completion of the circular course of my run, they are gone. I should have stopped. I feel shame as another scene flashes into my mind.

The thin fellow moves slowly through the crowd of people surrounding me. I have just finished the first section of my day-long workshop, and we are on a short break. It is going very well. The people are excited. The "recycle theology" experience is going better than I had hoped. We are brainstorming, and more than half of the people have come up with fresh, creative ideas. The thin fellow is working his way closer and closer to me.

The quick snatches of conversation are darting in every direction as people touch me and make comments. He is now waiting to speak while I exchange reactions with those milling around me. "May I speak with you?"

I manage to slowly rotate away from the others with responses designed to close down the conversations. We are now face-to-face. Others are turning away. "I used to serve a church in Washington County when you were working at the college. I was at the meeting where you asked those of us in other churches to support you. This was when you had been fired by the college for working with black students." He pauses and searches for his next words. "We didn't support you—I—wanted to do something. I—almost stood up and spoke on your behalf." There was a long pause. What does he want? I remember that church meeting well. Even my friends did not publicly speak up for me. I stood alone among the very people I had helped in many ways. They would not risk a personal affirmation.

In the safety of my present acceptance this timid pastor tells me about a time when he was afraid to publicly acknowledge me as a fellow worker. Should I rescue him or should I let him work it out himself? "I am sorry, man. I am afraid that it is your problem. You have to live with it."

Your heart knows that often you yourself have failed to support others. (Proverbs 7:22)

UNDER THE BLANKET

I stand under the shower for a long time. It feels so good to let the hot water roll over my body. I ran for two hours. Every muscle feels stretched and ready for relaxation. It feels so good when it's over—this doesn't apply just to hitting yourself in the head with a hammer. I look at the clock. It is two o'clock in the morning. I slip between the sheets. It is so cool and delicious. My body is exhausted to the point that I can feel all kinds of muscles I never noticed before. I yearn to stretch and stretch. The sheets are the clothing for my exercised naked body.

I couldn't believe the letter; yet I knew that it would come that day. I was in the midst of graduate work. I had spent seven years beyond college. I had passed graduate reading exams in six different languages and was well on the way to that doctor's degree and a life of teaching. However, one of the comprehensives stood in my way. I had failed to get the necessary B; C+ was the best that I could get. My last chance had come the week before. Now I held the news that I had again gotten the C+. I was finished. Everything was gone!

I walked around the empty apartment. Panic flooded

over me. How would I justify my failure to my wife? She had worked for the past five years to enable me to pursue my studies. What would I say to my friends? How could I face those who would be secretly pleased that I had failed?

I undressed and went to bed. I pulled the blanket over my head. I sobbed and sobbed. If I could only keep myself covered and away from the reality that could not be changed! There was something comforting about being wrapped in that blanket. I put the pillow over my head to shut out the noise of the city.

My body and intellect may fail, but God is always the security blanket for my mind and grades. (Psalm 73: 26)

THE FAMILY LOAF

It is 20 degrees, and my breath hangs in the air before me as I puff my way around the 1.2 mile course. Each step is painful. My right heel is hurting again. I know that it will work itself out in a couple of miles if I can just hang in there. The sharp pain shoots through my body with each step.

Lee Miller sits across from me in the small motel room in Louisiana. Outside it is hot and muggy. The air conditioner groans in the background. This creative writer and teacher is kindly sharing her story with me. Lee is one of those persons who became a victim of arthritis at an early age. Her medical advisors have been experimenting with exotic drugs to help her through the pain caused by the maze of complications that contribute to the disintegration of her health. Unfortunately, their medical brews have brought more pain and problems. Her skin has turned dark brown, and there is swelling in her body.

She refuses to give in to pain. Lee has just led an all-day workshop for local religious teachers. Several manuscripts await her return to the office.

We share. Our conversation focuses on the meaning of

the Lord's Supper. "My illness has given me a deeper understanding of the Table. The breaking of the bread takes on special meaning in the light of my pain. The significance of Christ's pain as our means to salvation is real to me."

We talk on and realize that we will soon be parting. "I will see you at the Table next week, Dennis."

"Unfortunately, Lee, where I worship they will not celebrate the Lord's Supper next week."

"I know. However, I have a covenant with the people I love. Whenever one of us takes Communion, we do it for the others. I will take it for you. We are the communion of saints. The Table links us together always."

This is my body, torn for you. (I Corinthians 11:24)

BABY FACE

*The woman explodes through
the grocery store doorway. Her cart is brimming with
food. Five children spill out from behind, beside, and
in front of her. The yellow newspaper van swings in front of
me. George is in the midst of his speedy delivery to the
newsstand. I jump over the curb and use the sidewalk for
several hundred yards. I find myself in the midst of the
shopping-cart lady and her brood. They look at my gold
sweat suit very carefully. I wave as I step around their little
bodies. One boy is on the brink of saying something: "Look
at the big yellow cheese!" They all break into gleeful
laughter.*

There was a certain status to
be gained by working in a shoe store during my high school
days. When I dropped by the homes of girl friends I could
pacify the nosy little brother with a handful of shoe store
suckers.

Our store was informal and busy. We were encouraged to
entertain and kid the customers. A lot of young girls came
in for this kind of attention from the salesmen.

We also sold children's shoes. No one wanted these
customers. We would turn them over to the assistant

manager. He was older and knew how to soothe and please the mothers.

One day I was hooked with a mother and child because it was my turn. The woman wanted shoes for her active three-year-old son. He wiggled, twisted, and turned. "No, no, no." He didn't like his new shoes. He wouldn't walk on them. I gave him a sucker. He threw it across the room. The lowest blow came when he turned and hit me with his fist. "Dear, don't hit the nice man in the stomach." I wanted to scream in my pain, "Lady, I wish he had hit me in the stomach!"

My patience was wearing thin. His mother told me that she could not see without her glasses and had better look for them. She turned away from us and started rummaging through her bag. My chance had come. I firmly held the child's foot and made a gross monster face at him. He was silent as he drew back in fear.

I turned to the mother. She was looking at me with her eyeglasses firmly in place. She turned to the child and said sweetly, "Don't be afraid just because the nasty man makes faces at you, dear."

A vicious person makes a violent face, but a caring person smiles. (Proverbs 21:29)

SISTER, SISTER

I am just about to beat the hill. Only a few more steps, and I will be able to burst down the other side. Suddenly my eye catches two figures stretched out on the grass. There is something about their intensity and rapport that reminds me of Nadine.

It was late. Our dates had returned to their homes. I had dropped off Abby at her doorstep. Nadine's date had taken her home. Here we were. Two friends. She's the closest thing to a sister I have ever had. She felt the same way about me as a brother. It was so comfortable to be close to someone without the fear and uncertainty that goes with becoming lovers. I needed her perspective as a woman. I know that she appreciated my unprejudiced viewpoint as a man.

The fireplace crackled, and the flames from the logs danced high in the air. But it does not bring us the kind of pleasure one might expect. We were both very low. Abby was preparing to dump me. I felt it in my bones. Nadine was talking about her guy. He had been very cruel and had disgraced her at her own party. She was sitting on the floor. Her eyes welled with tears. "Oh, Dennis, Dennis—" She

turned and put her head on my knees. I gently stroked her hair. For that moment we were brother and sister comforting each other.

A friend loves in all circumstances, and a brother/sister is given for moments of pain. (Proverbs 17:17)

I WANT YOUR BODY

As I hit the row of shops along my running route, I come upon three young women with fantastic bodies and tight-fitting jump suits. They are stopping shoppers and offering them black buttons. I can see that they are promoting the opening of a new health spa. When I come within three feet of them, I can finally read the buttons they are wearing: I Want Your Body.

It had been one of those amazing weekends. Something special had happened. It was more than the material I had prepared for the two hundred young people. It was true that they had been enabled to do many things. A Florida storm had forced us into the one-room building. The cold weather had pulled us together.

The last two hours together were focused on a worship celebration in which we shared the media gifts we had created during our time as a community. The service concluded with the bread and juice. Our love feast was called into being by the commission of Christ. We were at his Table. The community gathered around several tables. Each setting featured a different kind of bread. We gave thanks, broke the loaves, and ate and drank.

"We will never be together again in this configuration

until we gather in the kingdom of God. This is a foreshadowing of the eternal Table."

The kiss of peace for one another became a clustering and parting of tearful folk. As I stood at the Table, the kids came forward and hugged me. Others stroked my beard. Some kissed me. One girl put a seashell in my hand. I felt as if I were drifting. For just a second I perceived the kingdom of heaven which is now. We were loving one another for the journey and trials ahead.

Greet those in the fellowship with the kiss of love. (I Peter 5:14)

SMELL HOW
GOOD IT IS

I am tired. Just one more lap
and I will have had my twelve miles of running for today. It
is hard going. I let my senses carry me. I listen for what I
have been missing. "Click, click, click." My crazy right leg
is sending out its usual crackling sounds. I breathe deeply.
The extra oxygen gives me an added bit of energy. I can
also smell my sweat. Got to wash my running clothes. My
tongue explores my lips and the inside of my mouth. It is
funny how you can taste dryness. It will be super to pour
the cold water from the refrigerator down my throat. What
have my eyes missed during my previous passes of this bit
of scenery? The supermarket windows are plastered with
ads. There is a special on lemons. I didn't notice that
before. Lemons have always had a particularly strong hold
on me. I love to eat them, rind and all.

My days in Sidney were
busy. Every moment of my Australian trek had been filled
with teaching, talking, and celebrating. The lemon trees of
Sydney fascinated me. I had never been around growing
lemons. It was the time of year when the lemon season had
passed. At least, my host's backyard tree had dumped its
fruit on the ground. The yellow objects surrounded the

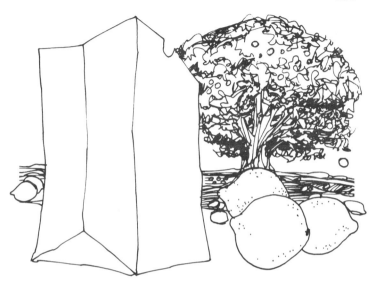

short tree. We were on our way to a Baptist church. I was to lead a Sunday morning class with 150 young men. I got a bag from the house and filled it with the bruised and discarded lemons.

The huge room was filled with students. They were curious about their guest teacher. The man who introduced me didn't help me overcome my nervousness. "Mr. Benson is from America." That was one strike against me. "He is here to show us how we should have Sunday school." Strike two.

I knew that the young people had been heavily exposed to the British educational influence in which the cognitive approach is stressed. Creative or experiential learning does not receive high priority. On the other hand, things aren't much different in the American educational system.

I decided to throw them onto their own resources. I read

Isaiah 53 about the Suffering Servant's being bruised and not highly accepted. The kids were then divided into small groups. I gave each unit a lemon from my bag and told them to pass it around. Each person was to share in what ways this piece of fruit was like the Messiah, or Jesus.

I held my breath. The room was totally silent. After two or three minutes the sound level began to rise. It got louder and louder as the young people entered into the process.

After five minutes, I called the class back to order and went from group to group while members shared what had been said in their groups. The comments were fine. At one small group, a young boy said: "I feel like the lemon because I am a Christian. In my school, becoming a Christian meant losing all my friends." Before we could respond, an older boy across the room spoke out. "Hang in there, mate. They may abuse and laugh at you now for your faith, but Christ will carry you through. Soon they will turn to you again because of your love and strength."

It was a beautiful morning. The kids were warm, intelligent, and creative. At the end of the session, one boy said, "Just smell this room! It smells like lemons! It is the smell of Christians being together in love!"

Live in love, just as Christ loved us and surrendered himself as a fragrant gift to God. (Ephesians 5:2)

I WANNA HOLD
YOUR HAND

Another hill. It is hard to take the Pennsylvania countryside at a run. Perhaps the inclines are more of a mental than a physical strain. I will make this one hill in good fashion. Oh, oh. There is a stalled car in the middle of the road. I want to run past it. However, I won't be able to pass by the other side. People might think that those who are jogging or running are available for information or aid. At least, we seem to be doing nothing very important.

Fortunately, the car is a compact import. I wave to the driver behind the wheel. I dig in and start pushing. It actually moves pretty easily. He is rolling now. He lets out the clutch and the car sputters to life and is quickly out of sight. With my hand prints on his trunk. I feel suddenly exhausted as I trot on and look at my dirty hands.

I had been in the room for several days; and yet I was still frightened. A seminary student shouldn't feel so insecure. Was it that I had polio, or was it merely being committed to a contagious-disease hospital that gave me this fear?

The big day finally came, and several relatives arrived at the doorway of my room. I had been in isolation for two weeks. They lingered at the door and looked in without entering. A wall of rejection seemed to separate the fearful, dear people at the door and me. Who could blame them? I wouldn't feel too comfortable with me either if I had been them. I had been out of touch with the living. Disappointment and loneliness uncontrollably overwhelmed me.

Dad broke through the moat of isolation by walking into the room. He sat on the edge of my bed and warmly shook my hand. Through his touch, he communicated to his son, "You are my son, and nothing can cut me off from loving you at this moment."

The touch of his hand made me realize the warmth of his gift and the huge cost of fear he must have paid to give it.

Touch me, and examine my hands; put your hand in my wound. (John 20:27)

THREE KISSES

The silver station wagon speeds past me, throwing up stones from the road. The adults are smoking and engrossed with the decision of where to go in the shopping center parking lot. They screech to a halt at the stop sign and wildly gawk for their destination. They are easy for me to dislike. However, the two small children in the back seat look at me as I run up behind the car. I wink at them. They break into huge smiles and wave at me. I give them my Rocky greeting and they clap.

"Deanna is a Mongoloid. This means that she will remain a child. She is very, very open and friendly. Sometimes this makes you think that she has something that we don't have. A couple of weeks ago we were walking down the street near her dad's office, and there she was saying, 'Hi, hi,' to everyone. Since I, her mother, am of the standard school, I sort of walked ahead of her a couple of steps. I didn't want people to think that this was coming from me.

"I could see out of the corner of my eye that a woman reacted. She bent over and kissed Deanna. I said: 'Hey, Deanna, how about that? You got a kiss out of that.'

"The woman said, 'Not only one kiss, but three. One for the Father, one for the Son, and one for the Holy Ghost.' This set Deanna up. She beamed all over. This is part of the baptism service, and she often goes around saying, 'In the name of the Father, Son, and Holy Ghost.' "

Placing a child in the middle of them and snuggling the babe, he said, "Whoever welcomes such a child in my name, welcomes me." (Mark 9:37)

THE BEST THAT I GOT

I have just started into the ninth lap around the quarter-mile track when superjock comes speeding by. I have seen the type before. He is my age, but his track clothes make him look like an Olympic competitor. He runs like he is out to take on the field. He is amazing to watch. His stride is long and smooth. There are power and skill in every move. It is now hard for me to accept my lumbering gait. He will soon lap me again.

Mose Henry sits in a small room. He is sharing his music with me. His full, rich voice reveals his professional background. The smiling children clap their hands outside the open window at the conclusion of his song. He smiles and waves at them.

They bear witness to the fruit of his work and love. He writes music for people as a man of faith. He speaks about the criticism he has received from a local pastor concerning his church music: "This guy argues that we should give God the best that we have—Bach, Beethoven, or Mozart. I say no. Man, God wants you! You must give him the best that you are." Tapping his guitar he adds, "Man, this is the best that I got."

During my run a teacher has had his high school class on one of the bleachers in the stadium. The students have been dismissed. My superjock friend has finished lapping me and has headed for the shower. I am discouraged and ready to stop short of my planned run. The teacher has now turned to watch me run. Just as I pass the place where he is sitting, he calls out, "Hang in there." A rush of new energy fills me. I complete my run, giving it the best that I've got.

Call out encouragement, and support one another just as you are doing. (I Thessalonians 5:11)

GET 'EM UP,
GET 'EM UP

It takes me an hour to decide whether to go running. Part of me feels spent; yet my addiction goads me on.

As I hit the pavement, things still don't feel very good. I wonder how I can complete the miles of my trek when I am exhausted already. The blast from a car horn almost jolts me into a telephone pole. It can't be more than a foot behind me. The fool!

The green car pulls up even with me. A man on the passenger's side looks at me and shakes his head. After rolling down his window, he removes his juicy cigar. His puffy red face looks disapprovingly at me. "It's all wrong. Your stride is bad, kid. You'll get shin splints unless you lift those legs. Get 'em up, get 'em, get 'em up!"

He sucks on his cigar until he convulses into violent coughing. Tears fill his eyes as he gasps for breath. Then he starts laughing at me. Choking and giggling, he manages to rattle, "Get 'em up, kid, get 'em up."

Dad told me the story again last Christmas. "When I was fifteen years old I got my first job, as a day laborer. It was the construction job on a huge grain elevator installation on the Mississippi. The first day was a mess. They gave me a shovel and told me to scoop up the slimy mud being dredged from the river for the barge channel. The boss showed me how to handle the big coal shovel. Yet, every scoop resulted in half of the black river lava rolling back over me. I heard a mocking laughter. There was Polly. The huge Irishman always looked as if he were recovering from the liquid celebration of the night before. He certainly had a hangover personality. He told me that I was doing my job all wrong. Each word seemed to slap me. Several times that day he came by and gave me his stinging abuse about my work.

"I told the foreman that I had had enough of this work. 'So you want a cleaner job, kid? Bring your swimming trunks tomorrow.'

"The next day was quite a switch. He handed me a hacksaw and told me to dive into the muddy waters of the Mississippi. I was to cut off a row of huge bolts that had been used to hold the forms for the concrete pier. To my horror, I learned that the bolts were four feet under water! I would dive in and find the bolts with my hands. The water was too dark to use my eyes. After several strokes of the saw, I would sputter to the surface gasping for air. Many times Polly would be standing there laughing. This father of five seemed to have no mercy for me. 'Why don't you use your gills, kid?'

"The foreman just looked at me when I reported that I would not spend another day in the river. I would become wrinkled like a pickle after another eight hours of this work. 'I have an easy job for you, kid. You can help Polly.'

"In a few minutes my harsh tutor and I were on the roof of the twelve-story grain elevator. It was our job to clear the loose concrete from the top of this huge structure.

"I don't know if I was more frightened by the height or by Polly. I filled my bucket and crawled to the edge. It seemed like an hour before the contents were spilled over the side. Polly just watched me. 'Can't you do anything right, kid? Let me show you.' I filled the bucket.

"He wrapped the rope attached to the bucket around his arm. With swaggering strides he walked to the edge and hurled the tilted container over the edge. There was a sharp crack as the weight of the concrete snapped the rope.

"I was watching his face. His expression suddenly changed. His feet slipped on the loose gravel, and he went over with the bucket.

He didn't scream. His body just dropped the twelve stories to the ground. I never returned to the job."

Safer is an inexperienced youth than a veteran who will not listen to others. (Ecclesiastes 4:13)

WILD AND CRAZY GUY

It is good to get away from the highway. I am always nervous when drivers can see me, but I don't know who the stranger is in the dark of night. The empty expanse of the huge shopping center parking lot looms ahead. It should be a good run. The heat of the day has given way to the welcome cool of the evening. As I move toward the department store, I notice some movement around a car. There are three men standing next to the vehicle. Thy are shouting and acting in a crazy manner. The clatter of an empty beer can echoes across the lot. Gales of laughter follow. I run as far to the left of the scene as I can. They spot me. "Want to go to a little party, running freak? We can make you run fast."

As I reach the drive circling the mall, a police car pulls up to the partying high school students. Loud voices ring out, and the two men with flashlights have the boys leaning with their hands on the car.

When I return to the south side of the shopping center, the police are pulling away with the young men in their car.

I open the door to find the woman from down the street. She asks if I will do a favor for her. Her son has been picked up and committed to the psychiatric section of a hospital. "You two seem to get along well. Will you visit him?"

I already knew my friend's history. Jim had been a brilliant student at a midwestern university. He was found early one morning wandering on the lakefront without his clothes, proclaiming to all that he was the savior. Jim escaped from a mental hospital and returned home. Visits to several treatment centers followed. He has been diagnosed as manic-depressive.

The last time he had stopped by our home, Jim sang new lyrics to the record I was playing while talking to me. He was acting as if he were two different people at once. One was creatively dreaming, and the other was totally aware of reality.

He was sitting on a green couch in the recreation area of the hospital. Four or five patients sat around him in a drugged stupor. They just stared into space. Jim was talking and singing to himself. He offered a startling contrast. His eyes were engaging an invisible audience. As I sat down, he continued his rap by sweeping me right into it. It was a heavy theological trip. He was at one with the legions of holy people who had lived or been created by the whole human experience. He was filled with love as he worked and reworked the mystical ladder of holiness. While this conversation was going on, we also rapped about the present. He was distressed over the drug orientation of his doctors. "They want to dope me back into normalcy."

He had been picked up by the police because he was wandering on a Sunday evening and calling out to all about the love of life. I told him that a fearful world was not ready for this kind of meandering love. In fact, someone somewhere would hurt him for such outpourings. He sadly nodded. Jim knew that something had to change. His

sentences came in broken fragments with singing sand-
wiched between the thought segments. We were comfortable. The vibes were flowing between us. I enjoyed his wild
company more than most of the conversations at social
gatherings. He felt so deeply about love. He cared about
values and knew exactly what the real world was like. We
were swaying and rocking in a strange but authentic
rhythm. He was my brother, and we were probing the
universe together. Our symbiotic communion was totally
out of sync with this room of drugged patients. In fact, what
we were sharing would be madness to most. We looked,
acted, and sounded like two crazy people.

The crisis at the hospital centered around the fact that
Jim didn't want to take the medication that would stabilize

him. "It will kill part of me." Yet this was the only way he could be accepted by society.

When I got up to go, he said: "I love you. Not in the fag sense. I love you as a brother." We embraced, and he kissed my cheek. I knew that I was saying farewell to the friend I had known.

The next time Jim and I talked was on a bus coming back from downtown. He had his hair cut short and was wearing a dark suit and conservative tie. The hospital drug treatment had been successful. He took his medication daily and could actually sit still and carry on a single-faceted conversation. He now "fits in" with society.

It was a struggle for me. I still felt my love for Jim. Yet, I felt more comfortable with the other Jim. He is now only half a person. Loneliness sets in. I am now mad without his madness to meet mine.

Jesus has lost his mind! (Mark 3:21)

POTHOLES

Weather ravages the streets of Pittsburgh. I suspect that the road-maintenance people use chocolate to fill the holes in the roads. The potholes are unpleasant for those driving cars; they are painful to runners.

My mind is wandering in rich fantasy. I am not aware of where I am or of what I am doing as I round the corner near the grocery store. My left foot suddenly drops into space as I step into a pothole. In the attempt to keep myself from falling, I put my weight on the twisted ankle. The knifelike pain sears through me. I cry out and slowly limp in the hope that I have not broken or sprained the runner's best friend. When you jog, you realize that you are not in a body, you are a body.

This was a hard day. My early morning radio show was followed by a visit to a friend in the hospital, a rock interview, and a party. It is now 12:30 A.M., and I have one more interview to do. The record company invited me to the postconcert party for a famous rock group, and the interview should be dynamite.

The fashionable pub has private rooms for special parties like this. I meet a friend from another station at the door. He looks worried and distracted. "How's it going?" His eyes dart back and forth before he answers. "I'm checking people." I am tired, but he looks totally out of it. I slap him on the back and dismiss his strange behavior. He is part of the management at a rival radio station. The ratings have just come in with us on top of the rock pile. They are very low.

With the exception of four folk from WDVE, the sixty or so people are from the other station. Booze is flowing, and these people on the fringe of the music business are acting the way they think rock stars should. It is amusing how nonmusicians always play the role better than the real stars.

The food and drinks are keeping everyone high. I take a cola after much prodding from one of the hosts. It is 2:00 A.M. when the star appears. We quickly make arrangements to interview him. The record-promotion man wants me to do it right in the party room. This is a drag. I am always searching out the best recording conditions. Yet, I want to get the interview.

We sit together in a booth, and the talk goes well. The lead singer looks worked to death. Just too many days and nights on the road. He reaches inside for energy and gives me a good exchange. We pose for pictures, and he walks away to greet the others in the room.

I am just putting the top of my case down on the recording equipment when I realize that my friend from the door is standing near me.

I smile at him. "Thanks for the hospitality, man." His head begins to shake. The veins in his neck are distended. "I—I—I ought to break your recorder and mike. I—I—I am so angry. I could shove them down your throat!"

The shock of his anger hits me like a slap. I can feel his emotion in a physical way. It is so unexpected. I respond

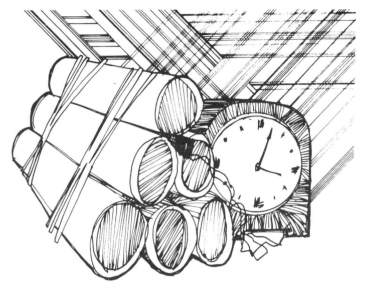

with concern and apology. This just fuels his wild emotions. "I—I—can't help myself. This is the way I am. I am so embarassed that you would interview him for your station at my party. I paid for this, and you do an interview!" Jimmy from our station joins us. I try to explain that it is not for the station. Nothing seems to help. The two of us are suddenly in a sea of angry, drunken faces. "Take his tape. Take his tape." Every word of apology from us just makes him worse. I turn and walk from the crowd. Another minute and there will be violence.

Instinctively, I quickly shift the interview tape from the tape machine to my inside pocket and replace it with an empty tape—just in case.

As I swing the car around in the street and head home, I am terribly disturbed by the pain of that moment. I haven't experienced such naked hatred and physical anger since the days of Selma. In the civil rights marches I saw how nonviolent love could change situations and people. I just didn't make it work in that bar.

I was powerless to defuse his anger. I guess that I am just too tired to be as sensitive as I should. It is easy to jar another's naked wound.

We are given the task of bringing hostile people together. (II Corinthians 5:18)

THE INVISIBLE WOMAN

The thaw has given us some relief from the cold spell but also pools of water. It is hard to run in this stuff. The trek along the highway is particularly unpleasant. The drivers roar past me at fifty-five miles an hour. They seem to not see me.

Each car throws sheets of water and slush at me. I can taste the road salt in my mouth. The invisible runner will be washed away by the spray of the cars.

Many sensations flow over me as I walk down the hall. The white paint and stainless steel make the odors even more distinctive. I am back in the hospital. After my chaplaincy experience, each visit to this special place brings a whirl of emotions. So many hours of life and death were spent with people in passage.

Today I am back visiting a twenty-one-year-old friend. He has had a series of operations. This is one of the most delicate. His eyesight is on the line. He has been fantastic in this struggle with the only real questions of life. He has given me much.

I peek into his room. His bed is empty. "He's gone back to intensive care." I thank his roommate and worry with each step over just what this turn of events means.

"He had three seizures this morning. It is lucky that his roommates were there." His mother sighs as she leans against my arm. She has been so strong and faithful through these years of danger and crises. "They forgot to prescribe the right medication!"

I talk with my friend. Then his mother and I go into the hall. I lean against the door frame as we talk. There is an old woman about forty feet away. I had noticed that the hospital people were helping her into a wheelchair as I arrived. They had a bottle connected to her intravenously that was hanging above her chair.

The mother and I huddle together as we talk in low tones. For thirty minutes we share the blessings of the successful surgery and crisis weathered. All this time I am facing the elderly woman down the hall. She keeps nodding to me. I nod back and continue my talking. Her eyes don't seem to leave me.

Suddenly, I notice something surrounding the old woman's chair. A shiny circle. There is a pool of blood on the floor! Before I can move a nurse also notices. A doctor soon appears.

The poor soul had been bleeding for the past thirty minutes, and no one had seen her. She had tried to signal me, but I did not understand her frantic message for help. I had been talking while this invisible lady splashed the floor with her blood.

A minister was in the hall, and he saw the needy person. Yet, he looked past her. (Luke 10:31)

MEAN STREETS

The park is a good place to run. At least, it was one of my favorite spots for a while. As I move along the road, I face traffic taking a shortcut through this wooded area. The speed limit is 15 miles per hour. However, no one pays much attention to such restrictions. The cars travel uncomfortably close to me at high speeds.

I notice that the drivers don't look very happy or very friendly. How can I transform these mean streets into something a bit different? I decide to wave at each driver. In the two-mile stretch, about forty cars pass me. The first day only three folk refuse to wave back or acknowledge my greeting in some manner. Most also slow down after this close encounter.

After a few days, regulars greet me before I can wave. For a friendly toot of the horn I give them a two-arms-over-the-head salute. I become their Rocky.

Workers in heavy trucks and teen-agers become the warmest companions to this road runner. They call out words of encouragement.

"You're looking good."

"Hang in there."

There are still some who will not smile or acknowledge my greeting, but it is amazing how on a lonely street, strangers can become a community of sojourners.

Thank you for joining me. Hang in there.